Ulrike Laubner

# A Product Manager's Cookbook

**30 recipes for relishing your daily life as a product manager**

Bibliographic information of the German Library:

The German Library catalogs this publication in the German National Bibliography; detailed bibliographic information can be found on the Internet website: http://dnb.ddb.de.


© 2022 Ulrike Laubner

ISBN: 9783744802093

June 2017, First Edition

Production and Publisher: BoD – Books on Demand, Norderstedt


Layout and Graphics: Ulrike Laubner | Fotolia

Cover design: © Guter Punkt, München | iStock

Editor for the English translation: Allison Turner

# About the author

*Ulrike Laubner*, born in 1971, has studied clothing technology, economics, and marketing. For over 20 years, her focus has been on developing innovations and improving existing products in the product portfolio. What innovations can be made? What makes a customer buy a product? How can existing products become more profitable? As a product manager, she focuses on the benefits to customers. As an engineer, she seeks continuous improvements in product development, which makes for satisfied customers, improved quality, greater profits, and reliable processes. She believes that company success and enjoyable work are equally important.

Passionate about product management, Ulrike Laubner founded her own company in 2011.
Today, as the owner of Corimbus GmbH, she advises companies on product management and on market introductions for new products. The company name, Corimbus, comes from the Latin word corymbus, referring to a kind of blossom. Labour should yield its fruit and with the right interplay of methods, knowledge and teamwork, it will.

Ulrike Laubner is an experienced product management consultant, trainer for product management on the "Open Product Management Workflow™" and author of many articles on the subject, and lecturer.

# How this book will help you relish your job

If you are reading this book, you want to change things. You want to become more efficient at product management. Whatever your position on the product management team, you're hoping to learn new techniques to use as the competition heats up.

You can read the book from cover to cover, or only the parts that interest you right now. You'll get insider tips for **developing products more quickly** without losing your momentum. You will learn methods for **better understanding your customers** and techniques for **decision-making**. You will find suggestions about **profitably designing products** and **introducing them into the market**. You will get proven **tips for all kinds of communication** that will ensure smooth cooperation across departments.

If you're a young product manager or are on a new career path, this book offers you an overview of essential issues and helps you recognize stumbling blocks. Experienced product managers and managers will find new methods and approaches for improving the process.

At the end of the book you'll find a worksheet that you can use to determine your own first actions towards more product management fitness.

I hope my tips surprise you and motivate you to do things differently.

I hope you can implement the suggestions in this book in your work and benefit concretely from them.

Kind regards,

# Contents

*Your actions*

# What the symbols mean

Financial: increased revenues or cost savings $\quad$ $\$$

Time: time savings in the innovation process

Personal: tapping the potential of your methods and
yourself

Quality: optimization for products, marketing or processes $\quad$ $Q$

# 1. Marketing from the Customer's View

Q
$

How do customers rate your product, service or market presence? Marketing is the reflection of a company and its services. The first hello, the product design, business cards and brochures, the homepage and the user interface all make up the public image.

Your product will sell better if you develop both the product and the marketing from the point of view of your target customer.

**Put yourself in the customer's position:**

- What problem does the product solve for me?
- Does it trigger the 'wow effect'?
- Why would I buy the product or service?
- When would I recommend it?

Creative minds develop many 'cool' features. These features really are fascinating and magnificent—but are they what the customer needs? Focus on the client benefit and your competitive position. In the 21$^{st}$ century, emotional needs are becoming more crucial for sales. Customers are increasingly searching for sense, for a simple lifestyle, a retreat back to nature or family, friends, and love. Keep these values in mind when developing innovations and when marketing them. Do not waste development and marketing money on unremarkable products that hardly anyone will buy and that will not improve your image. Do not let a lack of time lead to ill-thought-out decisions and then to product flops.

*"I have the best ideas when I imagine that I am my own customer."*

*(C. Lazarus, Founder of Toys "R" Us)*

## 2. Evaluating Ideas - The Scoring Method

You have analysed the market, carried out a SWOT analysis and found opportunities for a new product or business area. You have brainstormed or used idea management to come up with several exciting new ideas, technologies or services. Now the product management process begins.

How do you now determine which idea is the best?

Many customers tell me that for most of their ideas, their decision to proceed is quite spontaneous: "Let's just start! Obviously not every idea is going to be successful."

But how long can a company afford these failures if the competition is faster and their product margins erode?

Statistics show that of the thousands of ideas out there, only 6% are successfully introduced into the market. Of course, there are various reasons for this, but one is that the product requirements have not been checked thoroughly. The product manager must analyse and assess new ideas systematically, so as to make a conscious and firm decision. Poor decision-making often leads to delays in the market introduction of a project. Good, conscious decisions are made with the four-step scoring method.

**The four-step scoring method:**

1. Develop company-specific assessment criteria from the perspective of the company, the customer, the employees and the competition
2. Identify the weight of each individual criterion
3. Evaluate each idea in a cross-departmental team
4. Identify the ideas with the highest number of points

Then check whether the idea matches the company strategy and the product objectives. For example, if the best idea is a new product that is manufactured with a high-tech plastic, it might contradict the company's sustainability strategy. Then the idea will have to be more closely analyzed in relation to the business objectives and strategy.

Example:

| Criteria | Rating | Product A | | Product B | | Product C | |
|---|---|---|---|---|---|---|---|
| | | Weight | Score (Σ) | Weight | Score (Σ) | Weight | Score (Σ) |
| New customer value | 5 | 2 | 10 | 5 | 25 | 5 | 25 |
| competitors' edge | 5 | 2 | 10 | 5 | 25 | 3 | 15 |
| innovation | 5 | 1 | 5 | 5 | 25 | 1 | 5 |
| sustainability | 2 | 5 | 10 | 3 | 6 | 5 | 10 |
| new target group | 2 | 0 | 0 | 0 | 0 | 5 | 10 |
| internal knowledge | 1 | 5 | 5 | 5 | 5 | 3 | 3 |
| profit potential | 4 | 1 | 4 | 5 | 20 | 3 | 12 |
| Total | | | 44 | | 106 | | 80 |

Rating: 1-5, 5 the highest
Weight: 1-5, 5 the most important

**The Scoring Method**

In this example, product b emerges as the best product. For market growth or profit reasons, it may make sense to develop product B, even though it is not as sustainable as other solutions. The final decision is also dependent on strategy fulfillment, project resources, skills as well as the financial situation.

If you have little time or are missing information, you may want to use a different technique to make decisions about new product variants or innovations. See Chapter 5: Make decisions confidently!

## 3. A General Dogsbody– A Product Manager's Core Tasks

I encounter many different types of product managers in the courses I teach. Since the title 'product manager' is not trademarked, the role seems to apply to many different fields of work. Employees in sales, distribution, purchasing and development are all 'product managers'. Is someone who is only concerned with the product during its life cycle really a product manager?

**A typical product manager has the following core tasks:**

- Market analysis and observation
- Development of new product ideas
- Creation of marketing plans (the 4Ps: product, price, place, promotion)
- Product specification, product briefings
- Market introduction of the product
- Product controlling
- Product care during the life cycle
- Product elimination (see chapter 18)
- Internal and external communication

**Tasks that product managers do not do:**

- Hotline support
- Homepage maintenance
- Collecting financial figures
- Creating advertisements
- Building design concepts
- Elaborating functional specifications (see chapter 7)

**Do you have tasks that do not fall under product management? Note them on the last page as room for optimization.**

# 4. Value Curves - The Product Life Cycle

 Every product and every service will have its peak sales period and its weak sales periods. In total, products go through five phases, each of which requires its very own marketing campaign.

1. Innovation phase
2. Introduction phase
3. Growth phase
4. Maturity phase
5. Degeneration phase

But how do you know what phase a product is in? How do you decide on the right marketing actions or on investing in new developments?

Look at figures for the product since its launch to find out whether the product can be eliminated, needs further development, or would benefit from a new advertising campaign. You can also make some assumptions based on the historical data of similar products.

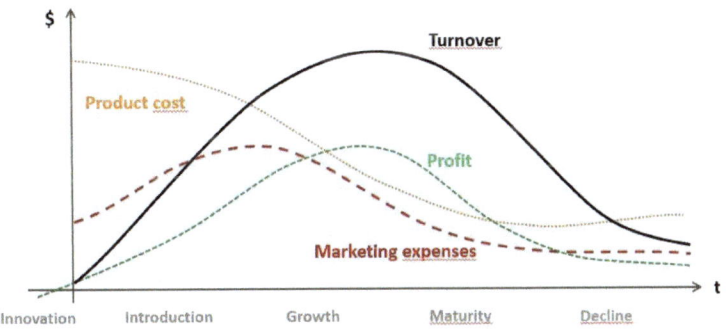

**The ideal product life cycle**

**Indicators of the state of the product life cycle:**

- Turnover and sales figures
- Contribution margin
- Marketing and sales expenses
- Development costs

These numbers are indicators of where a product currently is in its life cycle. Development costs are lower in the introduction phase than in the innovation phase, but the marketing costs for launching new products are high. In the maturity phase, yields are ideally high and marketing expenses relatively low.

However, these indicators alone do not tell the whole story. A slump in sales may also be due to the current economic situation. This means that to analyze the product life cycle curve you will need to make further observations, such as noting the arrival of a new competitor, changes in the exchange rate, and trends in the market.

## 5. Make Decisions Confidently!

*"It is better to make imperfect decisions than to always be searching for the perfect decisions that will never exist."*

*(Charles de Gaulle, 1890-1970).*

This sounds almost impossible to German and Swiss ears; we're too inclined to strive for perfect quality. But how much time passes before the right decision is made? Is it sometimes so long that the opportunity has come and gone?

**5 points for your decisions:**

1. Do not decide too quickly!
2. Get a second opinion.
3. What are the pros and cons?

4.   What alternative solutions can you find?
5.   How can you argue for your decision?

Imagine you are sitting at an intersection. You know the name of your destination. However, you do not know the way. You have to decide! If you just sit and wait rather than doing anything, watch how many other people will pass by and leave you behind. Even if it is the wrong way, you have to choose a way.
Be happy that you can make decisions, it is the only way you can progress!

If you cannot get all the information you need, follow your gut instinct. I have found that it continuously gets better with more experience. This intuition is especially helpful for experienced people when they do not have much time to make a decision. Use the 'follow your first impulse' method. Pay attention to the first thought that comes to you and check what feelings it triggers. If you decide against that idea, check the second one.

What if you have deliberated and still cannot decide? Ask yourself the 'disaster question' Which choice will cause the smaller loss if it turns out to be wrong? Decide on the solution that will bring the least damage, for example in the loss of image, waste of resources, and dissatisfaction of employees.

If the decision between two options is difficult for you, then ask yourself: "What keeps me holding on to this idea?" or "What draws me to it?" Then decide for the option with the stronger arguments.

"You cannot ride two horses with one butt."

(Woody Allen)

# 6. Spot Trends or Discover Needs

Companies are successful if they identify tomorrow's trends and implement them in customized products. They are successful because they are the first ones. The triumph belongs to the innovation leaders: the triumph of the margin, of the first buyer, of the higher turnover and of the good image.

If you are in the rare situation of being able to implement emerging trends and are seeking ideas for innovations, there are a wealth of sources you can regularly check. However, do not follow every trend. The only ones that are of value to your company are those that are useful to your customers and strengthen your competitive position.

**Sources for new trends:**

- Daily newspapers and journals (domestic and international)
- Future institutes and trend research
- Following product trends in related fields
- Customer and supplier conversations
- Discussions with personal and professional colleagues
- Cross-departmental exchange
- Buyer information
- Social changes
- Specialized and trade fairs
- Colleges
- Reports from business consultants

**Trend and future institutions on the internet:**

www.newbuildings.org(Buildings)
www.mckinsey.com/industries/high-tech (IT)
www.kivi.nl/english (Energy)
www.rolandberger.com/trend-compendium/tc2030 (various trends)

or view Alison Sanders TED talk on "Megatrends-The art and science of trends tracking."

Or would you rather be the trendsetter yourself? Then do as Steve Jobs or the makers of Nespresso did: ask yourself the following core questions: What can you do for your customers to clearly improve their quality of life, and what possibilities are there to make that happen? These thought experiments can lead to technological leaps. Groundbreaking innovations are ones that drastically change people's behavior, but few such products were predicted to be a trend. Such technological leaps include the invention of the wheel, the light bulb, the printing press, the computer, the smartphone, Nespresso, etc.

## 7. The Burden of Requirements Specification

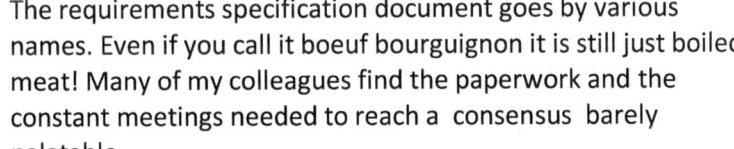

The requirements specification document goes by various names. Even if you call it boeuf bourguignon it is still just boiled meat! Many of my colleagues find the paperwork and the constant meetings needed to reach a consensus barely palatable.

The product specifications serve to keep everyone involved in developing the product on the same path to introducing a successful product in the market. The product specifications should be acknowledged as the bread-and-butter of successful product development.

The manufacturing costs of a product largely depend on this product definition. By taking enough time for product planning at an early stage of development, repeated corrections and fatal errors can be avoided and better solutions can be found. The better solutions may include the use of new materials and technologies, different construction methods, or new production processes that save production costs.

Horrendous rejection and reworking costs can eat up the product margins! How can you tell? Look at the number of complaints, the amount and type of quality costs, the number of guarantee claims, and the additional development efforts required.

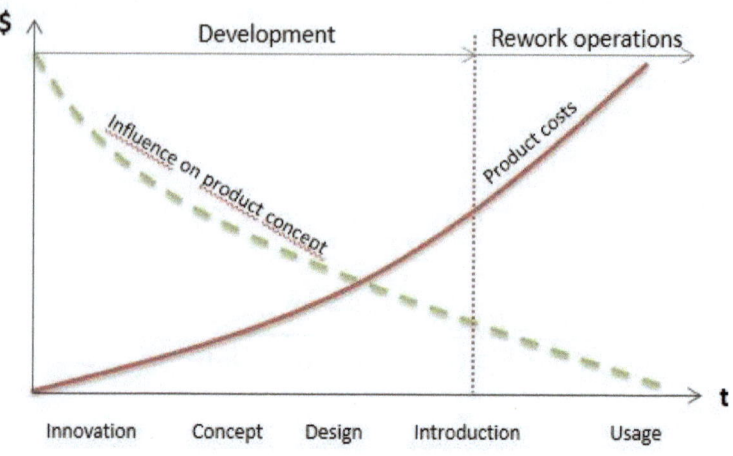

**How costs affect the innovation process**

In the real world, consequential costs are often top secret. There is no need to reinvent the wheel every time you do requirement specifications. Company standards and a documentation template help get the job done quickly and well. It is important not to miss any product components in the specification. The best is to create a checklist.

Please note that a requirements specification book is not a functional specification book. Since the two terms are often difficult to understand, the next table shows the differences.

|  | **Requirements Specification book** | **Functional specification book** |
|---|---|---|
| Synonyms | Market requirements Requirements catalog Requirements specification | Design Concept |
| Question | What is required? | How is it made? |
| Contents | Requirements for the core product and expanded product | Detailed description of all components and solutions |
| Creator | Product Manager | Developer, Designer, Engineer |
| Recipient | Developer | Production, Procurement Purchasing |

**Differentiation criteria for the requirements and functional specifications books**

**Sit down with your next specification with gusto:**

- Excerpt from marketing plan, i.e. launch countries, dates
- Product description
- Product target and characteristics
- Uses and process descriptions
- Integration of standard components
- Use of accessories
- Quality characteristics or numbers
- Design requirements, patents and property rights
- Operating instructions
- Packaging information

- Services
- Marketing action plan
- Product variant plan
- Target production price
- Budgeted sales figures
- Applicable laws and standards

**Your advantage:**

External suppliers and colleagues appreciate easy-to-understand specifications. Give them the most accurate information possible and a clear direction. This lets suppliers and colleagues deliver better results and make fewer mistakes with less effort on their side.

**Have you identified things to optimize in the requirements specification book? Note them on the last page with the actions you will take!**


## 8. Mastering your Workload – Time Management

How many projects are piling up on your desk – 7? 11? or more? Do you fall asleep easily or do you feel like a hamster on a hamster wheel?

One of my clients told me that he was working on 21 projects and that he did not know how to deliver the products to the customers on time: "There are new issues all the time. Customers keep imposing new requirements or want to discuss a product price after we've already agreed on it."

In this particular case, by improving the specifications and communication he was able to reduce his weekly work time by more than 20%. He gained 10 hours per week!

**Ways to save time:**

- Agree with the client on goals and make them binding
- Have binding specifications signed by all stakeholders
- Highlight the consequences for the deadline, quality, and price of every change request and record the decisions
- Take minutes during the meeting according to the TATVEO concept (topic, action, timeframe, valued actor, end result, open issues)
- Create checklists for all deliverables in the project
- Learn how to say 'No'
- Group similar tasks, reserve a slot in your calendar for them and work through the list
- Decline unnecessary meetings
- Create a work plan with priorities A, B, and C

Make checklists. Checklists improve both efficiency and quality by adding structure to your actions and keeping you from forgetting items.

Being disciplined about the documentation of new events or changes lets you avoid a time-consuming document search. These days, product managers enter new important information about a customer into a central system. The system tracks, for example, quality defects or order deadlines. But it does not replace any project documents or change requests. Anyone at the company who needs to can look at this 'notebook' and get an overview of the current status. This will save product managers 50% of the time that was otherwise wasted searching for information. Think about it: as a product manager, you do not get paid to manage data and search for product data! With a few improvements you can permanently reduce your catastrophic overtime hours. Try it out and enjoy your newly saved time.

# 9. Daily Business: S.O.S. Actions!

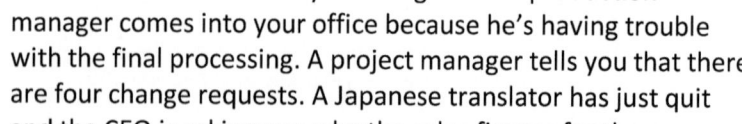

It is 10:30 on a Wednesday morning and the production manager comes into your office because he's having trouble with the final processing. A project manager tells you that there are four change requests. A Japanese translator has just quit and the CEO is asking you why the sales figures for the new product have not met the objectives. Your email inbox is overflowing. And so go 90% of a product manager's days. As a product manager, you are expected to find solutions immediately.

**Situations that call for immediate action:**

- Poor quality resulting in injury
- Increasing warranty claims
- Frequent customer complaints
- Sales figures not reached
- Market launch delayed

**Tips for S.O.S actions**

- Never communicate solutions before they're complete!
- Analyze the causes of problems with your team
- Take immediate action if the problem will take some time to fix. Communication is also an action!
- Plan the next steps for improvement
- Inform stakeholders about the approach you're taking

If the S.O.S. actions are similar or even always the same, optimize your process to fix the causes. This will eliminate many complaints, avoid increased costs, and prevent employee dissatisfaction. Customers, employees, and companies benefit from the process optimization in the long term.

# 10. Accurate Product Briefings for Agencies

"Wow, you created a great sample there. Downright genius as an initial sample!" "Yes, your presentation was very precise and we had a good understanding of what you need from us."

This is a dialog I encounter often, whether the briefings are about marketing, design, homepages, or prototypes. Excellent preparation saves valuable time and money for everyone involved. This is money that can be invested in new ideas or employees.

What it takes is a little calm and quiet time to prepare the briefing, and you'll save valuable time in the development process.

**What's in a product briefing**

- Information about the new design, relaunch or special model
- Background, starting point and goals
- List of products involved: the product portfolio, a single segment, or a single product
- List of related products, e.g. spare parts, accessories, user manuals, service manuals, packaging, courseware
- Compatibility
- Product variants
- Buyer group and purchasing decision makers
- Launch date and launch event
- Target product costs
- Sales price
- Budgeted sales figures
- International differences (e.g. logos, packaging, delivery range)
- Internal policies
- Corporate identity (CI/CD)

- Values: ecology, tradition, simplicity, etc.
- Relevant competing products

Price information gives developers an idea of the value, as well as of the possible technologies they can use. Keep in mind that you're giving out extremely sensitive information. Make sure a non-disclosure agreement is signed before passing on the information to externals.

Think about what information is needed to make the briefing easy to understand. Ask your suppliers what they need from you. This is how you get to a good win-win situation.

And keep your presentation to no more than two A4 pages!

## 11. Traveling with your Customers – The Customer Journey Map

Q "Our clients are satisfied. Sales are great." You are satisfied, but it could be better, couldn't it?

The customer journey is a check of the entire sales process. You are mentally going shopping with your customer. You will find out what he experiences at various points of contact with the company or the product. The journey begins when the customer first becomes aware of the company.

**Your journey with the customer could look like this:**

- Get information from your own professional network
- Get information in B2C from family and friends
- Make inquiries by phone, by email, and at sale points
- Read websites, brochures, flyers, and social media
- Assess the delivery of products and services
- Assess the after-sale actions

At each contact point, ask the customers how they felt i.e. valued, well informed, or perhaps not understood and whether they were satisfied with what they received i.e. information, product, service.

A major clothing manufacturer has recently changed its payment method to online payments for all delivery customers. Customers who prefer a more traditional method can instead print out a payment slip from the homepage. The deposit slip has to be perfectly cut for it to be accepted by a financial institution for processing. If this is not the case, it must be trimmed. Are the customers really satisfied with this? What are financial institutions becoming, if their employees must be «scissors virtuosos»?

The customer journey map clearly shows where there is potential for effective improvements in communication, customer processes, marketing, and the product itself. Try it with your current customers. When making innovations, follow the journey from a customer perspective with various colleagues, especially those outside of marketing.

## 12. Getting to know the Customer – The Persona Method

Product purchases are decided by people – real people, not anonymous target groups. The character portrayed for product creations is called a 'persona'.

When my developer colleagues came to me with a clever idea, I would ask: "Who is this intended for?" "For everyone" was the enthusiastic answer. But, sometimes a young, enthusiastic woman customer will have different expectations of a product than an older and wiser man.

'Personas' give you deep insights into clients' ways of thinking and typical behavior. Developers, marketing executives, or purchasers can specifically carry out their activities from the perspective of the 'persona'.

**Example: A coffee machine persona:**

**Basic needs** for the product: She wants to shine in front of her family. She does not want to 'look stupid' when using the new coffee machine. She wants no noise.

**Professional and personal environment:** She works in an open space office with a coffee machine. She meets friends after work. She enjoys spending her free time with family and friends. She is active in her free time and visits a café twice a week.

**The person's character**: Everything must be quick. Life is to be enjoyed. She is goal- and status-oriented, and eco-conscious.

**Product-relevant personal data**: She lives in Munich. She is 38 years old, female, and has two kids. She owns two coffee machines. She drinks three cups of coffee per day and enjoys a coffee in the evening. Every Sunday morning, she goes to a jazz café, where she reads the newspaper and drinks a latte macchiato. She does not buy coffee to go.

A typical **name**: Kathy

**Description** of the persona: appreciates coffee

**Face:** characteristic image of the person

**Description:** 1 A4 page

Names like 'Kathy', 'Peter', or 'Kevin' create images and everyday scenarios in our heads. "We have developed an amazing idea for Kevin" or "Our customer, Martha, is having trouble using the product." What are you thinking about now? Are you imagining Martha at home, knitting? And is Kevin gaming right now?

A picture is worth a thousand words. Hang up this persona picture in every department and talk about it in presentations, reports, briefings, etc. You'll see how quickly it creates a consensus among the different departments.

**Persona**

**Product:** *Sample Food*

**Name:** *S. Ample*        **Gender and age:**        **City and Country:**
**Job position:**            **Education:**

**Story according to the product/usage/problems:**

**Roles in job and private life:**                    **Characteristics:**

**Values:**

**My motivations?**                                    **What does upset me?**

**Main goals in life?**                                **What kind of media do I use/read?**

**Where do I inform myself upon new products?**

Persona data sheet

### A 10-minute exercise in persuasion:

Select a product i.e. a bike/smartphone/TV that everyone knows and first ask question 1. Then show a portrait photo with question 2.

1. What needs does our customer from target group x have? He is 35 years old, divorced, lives in London and makes 4000£ a month. What is important to him about the product?

2. What is important to Markus about the product? He's 44 years old, an engineer, likes traveling, loves nature, goes to the gym three times per week and likes to ride his bike in the summer. He likes pragmatic solutions. His

bike was stolen three times. His life motto: You only live once.

You will notice that the answers to question 1 come very hesitantly but they gush from the respondents for question 2. Without knowing the customer and their needs and problems you can hardly find the right requirements for the products. They would be a costly guess.

## 13. Offline is OUT – Online is IN

When I was looking for a printing service for the present book, I found an interesting company on the internet. I looked for a contact form, email address or an offer calculation tool to get answers to my questions. I was hoping to have my questions answered the next morning. There was only a phone number. It was 10:30 pm when I saw this. What do you think? Was this the company that printed my book?

80% of all businesses know that digital marketing is important, but less than 40% implement it. Why? We all search for information online! Daily, or hourly. Why wouldn't this go for customers as well? Social media is used by 42% of all companies in the German-speaking area, mobile websites by 30% and digital magazines by 28%.[1]
Ask your customers how they search for information and find out what social media they use.

**How can you be found online?**

- With what search terms can you be found on Google?
- Can you in fact be found?
- Do you use social media?

---

[1] Corporate Publishing Study III: The role of digital media in the CP-Mix, zehnvier GmbH und EICP, 2013 (German)

- How can customers contact you?
- How can customers recommend your product?

**Make it easy for your customer to find you:**

- With a simple structure and easy navigation
- With up-to-date contact options
- With postings, mailings and tweets that show you as an expert
- With a current company description on social media

# 14. Meetings – "Lord of the Things"

How many hours do you spend in meetings?
I have had weeks with 20–35hours of meetings. "Do you ever work?" was only one of the comments from my family. "Yes, of course, we discuss, find solutions, vote and make important decisions." Sometimes I doubted my statement as soon as I made it: Are we doing well, or can this enormous number of hours be reduced?

You can assess the success of a meeting by the points discussed and the time taken. With a systematic approach, you can keep a cool head even during hectic times, reach your meeting's goal and actually increase meeting quality while saving time.

**10 tips for efficient meetings:**

1. Only invite people who can contribute
2. Prepare the agenda, indicating limited speaking times
3. Send invitations via Outlook or Lotus Notes
4. Include information with the invitation
5. Prepare the room and check the equipment in advance
6. Make sure all the speakers are prepared
7. Start meeting on time and chair assertively
8. Pay attention to the speaking times and save open issues for later

9. Take minutes according to the TATVEO concept (topic, action, timeframe, valued actor, end result, open issues)
10. Send the minutes within 24 hours of the meeting

With a disciplined approach, you can easily save 5–8 hours per week. Questions, ambiguities, and misunderstandings will be reduced to a minimum. Decisions and incomplete actions are logged and readily available for checking.

How do you feel about meetings at your company? Have you identified potential improvements?

## 15. Managing Product Projects –Focus on the Goal

I often hear developers say "We cannot plan our products exactly because we do not know everything." This is the crux of the problem with projects.

*In the 5th century BC, Confucius said: He who knows the goal, can decide. He who decides finds peace. He who finds peace feels safe. He who feels safe can reflect. He who reflects can improve things.*

And that's the point. Anyone who wants to achieve real successes in innovation projects needs to know what the customer wishes to spend his money on. This is true whether it is an internal customer (e.g. with process improvements) or the purchaser of your product.

Precisely define the quality, the financial objectives, and the benefits for the customers as well as the design, technology, and marketing requirements. This will give you clear guidelines towards the goal, so that everyone is heading in the same direction. You notice when you get off track and you can steer your way back. If you do not know your goals, you will not make decisions and you will not move forward at all.

40% of innovations fail due to the lack of decisions among leaders.[2] This alarming number can be reduced significantly with a clear goal orientation and prioritizing functions on customers' needs.

**Defining S.M.A.R.T. goals:**

**s**pecific, **m**easurable, **a**mbitious, **r**ealistic, **t**ime-bound

Take the time at the beginning, both within the team and with the client, to define precise goals and to set measurement criteria.

**Compare the effects of two goal definitions:**

1. "The new car must be better than the best Audi model!"
2. "Our new luxury class car combines high energy efficiency, trendy design and smart technology for 20% more safety on the road, and will be introduced in the USA, Germany, and Switzerland on 03/31/2015 for €37,000."

Notice the difference?
In example 2, you know that you need to look for energy-efficient technologies or materials. You will choose designers whose trademark is trendiness and who build in future-facing electronics. You know exactly the direction you have to head. Example 1, on the other hand, either forces you to ask a lot of questions or to start by making assumptions. Please avoid the latter in any case.

---

[2] Study by Planview, Inc., 2013, www. Planview.de

A study at the Technical University of Berlin[3] shows that many companies complain about the lack of consequences for decisions that crash projects (67%), duplicated work (32%) and a distribution of resources that does not conform with strategy (34%).

You can influence this in the future. Have the courage to question the goals behind your orders. Do not start as soon as you receive a task, but make sure that you have a clear vision of the project objectives.

## 16. Living a Multi-Cultural Communication

I was a communication philistine at the beginning of my career: I proceeded on false assumptions. Today, communication is one of the most valuable building blocks of my company. Keep reading if you have ever had a 'bloody nose' yourself!

As a product manager, you communicate internally with the development department, production, purchasing, sales, technology, marketing, finance, quality control and management. And your communication does not stop at the company door. Suppliers, customers, distributors, competitors, trade fair visitors, and others are waiting for you. They move in different hierarchies and cultures.

Whenever you think "Man, he does not get it! It'll take three times as long if I have to explain it. I'll just do it myself," think about what you can change.
It is much easier to change your own behavior than to motivate others to change, so look at your communication.

---

[3] An empirical investigation on how portfolio risk management influences project portfolio success, International Journal of Projectmanagement, Volume 31, Issue 6, August 2013, J. Teller, A. Koch

**Communication for cooperation:**

- Be honest with yourself and others
- Admit errors
- Share information accurately
- Make the information suit the recipients
- Address conflicts as soon as they arise
- Keep written communication as short as possible
- Communicate about errors proactively
- Have a positive attitude towards others
- Show your appreciation for others' cooperation

Ask your counterpart if and how they have understood you. A Polish CAD engineer will have a different understanding than a Chinese supplier and then you. Keep this in mind in your written and oral communication and avoid misunderstandings due to language barriers and different mindsets.

The reward for your professional communication will be noticeably better cooperation and your reputation among colleagues and management.

**Can you think of ways to improve your communications? Write your plan on the last page.**

# 17. The Buyer as a Friend - Teamwork

Imagine the following situation: You urgently need a new sample. You fill out the necessary form and ask the buyer personally to place an order. You leave the department with your head hanging low. What happened?

The purchasing department has to seek 2–3 offers, the ordering times are longer, or the supplier does not fit your portfolio. And your company wants to bring an innovative product to the market! Product managers complain: "No wonder we're always too late with our innovations." 56% of all companies actually miss their market launch deadline.[4]

Just like product development, purchasing also requires processes to ensure quality and customer satisfaction. The processes are not there to annoy the dedicated product manager. The purchasing department wants what you want: the best possible product at the best price, of the right quality and by the optimum deadline.

Treat the buyer as your friend. Like you and me, he wants to be appreciated for his work. Things will go smoothly if you understand his tasks and regularly talk to him. The buyer is at the pulse of the times. He knows the supplier market, participates in fairs and learns about new technologies. This gives him valuable insider knowledge and access to useful suppliers so he gets his samples more quickly. You'll find that buyers come to you with brilliant ideas if you let them. And how proud they'll be if one of their ideas is implemented with a product.

**Encourage teamwork**

Integrate the purchasing department into projects and preliminary studies early on. That way, everyone profits from everyone else's knowledge. The product manager knows the purchasing processes and can make his needs known earlier if possible. At the same time, the buyer knows about new things coming up and is not thrown in at the deep end, where no one can perform at their best.

---

[4] Study by Planview, Inc., 2013, www.planview.de

# 18. Death of a Product: Eliminating Products

 With almost all products, there comes a time when sales decrease in the long term or stagnate at a low level. Such a product has to be eliminated. But the task of eliminating products is often neglected. The ongoing projects for new products and best-sellers are more urgent and attractive. However, unprofitable products generate storage and customer service costs for the product and its accessories, care costs, and the need for spare parts to remain available. Have the courage to question even long-time bestsellers if their sales figures can no longer be increased.

**How can you recognize the death of a product?**

- Sales figures are consistently low
- Storage costs are higher than the product yields
- Fixed costs are not covered
- The in-house cost is greater than the profit
- No customers with a particular use for the product
- The product serves only as a reason to buy other products
- Market growth is declining

**How to manage your product cleanup:**

- Analyze the market growth and market share
- Analyze the impact on other products!
- Argue for your decision
- Work with sales and procurement to plan the phase-out
- Keep warranties and spare parts for the stock in mind
- Communicate the phasing out of the product both internally and externally
- Offer sales clear-out promotions for the product and their  accessories
- If necessary, provide replacement products

## Sales Output

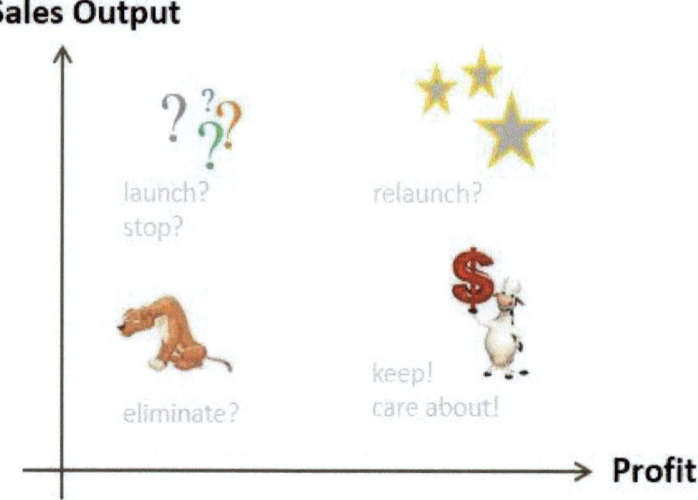

**Is it still worth selling the 'poor dogs'?**

### Risks associated with the product cleanup:

Analyze the positioning of the products in your portfolio before the product cleanup. Removing a strategically important product from the product line may trigger the loss of sales of other products. For example, if an inexpensive old product from the range serves as a sales help for other products with larger margins, then removing it from the range will most likely reduce the sale of these products. This can lead shopkeepers to opt for a competing product, and your sales to decrease even more.

Avoid these risks by comparing the savings in internal costs and complexity with the impact on sales of eliminating a product.

# 19.Preparing a Successful Product Launch

The project is complete. The product will be launched and your company is waiting anxiously for the first reactions. And then it happens: customers or shopkeepers complain that the product quality is bad, the packaging falls apart, the delivery time is too long, the software navigation is confusing or the production cannot keep up with the demand.

How to avoid negative experiences with the market launch? Not every obstacle can be eliminated in our networked world of global customers and suppliers. Unrest or environmental disasters cannot be integrated into the planning. But risks such as poor quality of products, delays or damages in delivery or products that customers find unacceptable can be identified in advance.

**10 tips for a successful product launch:**

1. Use interdisciplinary project-planning teams
2. Prioritize customer benefits
3. Be frank about the consequences of new changes
4. Integrate procurement, marketing and sales at an early stage
5. Set quality indicators and actively control the quality
6. Perform regular product testing with users and vendors
7. Analyze risks at an early stage and mitigate them
8. Plan launches by countries and quantities per country
9. Train sales management and team promptly
10. For critical suppliers and processes, have the quantities you expect to need produced in advance.

For highly uncertain product launches, you can introduce the products in test markets, 'Lead Countries'. Allow a set time period to make improvements to the product and in the communication and only then introduce the products in other countries.

Look at the well-known product recalls by car manufacturers. Toyota recently recalled six million cars around the world. The costs they incurred show the need for a careful product and market introduction at the beginning of a project.

## 20. Scanning the Horizon – Benchmarks

Companies require extensive data about competing products. A benchmark allows you to systematically compare your company with the best in its industry. This means analyzing processes, business models, products, technologies, or marketing to uncover opportunities for new competitive advantages.
In the following example, you see a benchmark between three companies (red, green, blue) with their products (D, P, B). The size of the circles represents the market share.

The example shows where the company's products' quality and price are, compared with its competition.

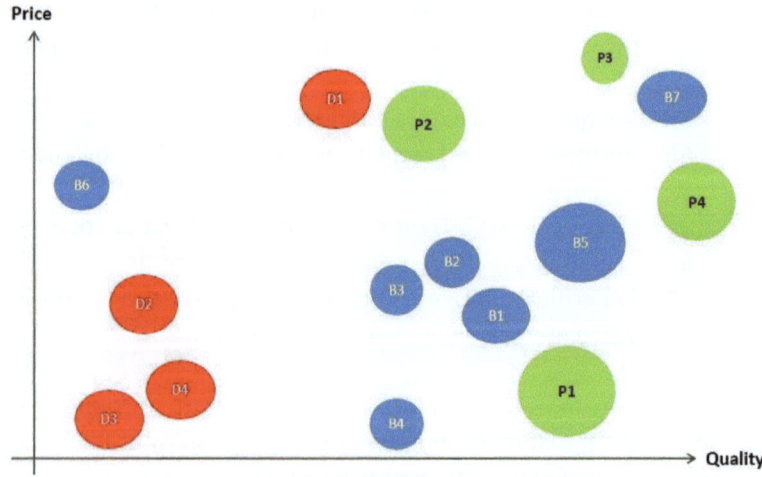

**Product positioning in the market**

How do you get this data?

Take advantage of your networks with the competition, colleagues and contacts in other companies, customer surveys and sales staff to get this information. Get your competitors' marketing material, analyze their homepage and buy competing products. Keeping up good relations with the supplier networks pays off when you want to buy competing products that are not yet available in your country.

**The right time for a benchmark:**

- Continuously
- When relaunching your own product
- When a competitor launches a product

**And how else can you use a product benchmark?**

You now know the strengths and weaknesses of your product compared to the competition. Put this information together for your field sales force and your dealers. They will be delighted to have new arguments for the strengths and benefits of the product and will also be better prepared to dispute the weaknesses.

# 21.Modern Design – A feast for your eyes

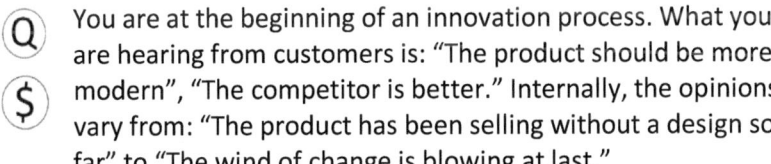 You are at the beginning of an innovation process. What you are hearing from customers is: "The product should be more modern", "The competitor is better." Internally, the opinions vary from: "The product has been selling without a design so far" to "The wind of change is blowing at last."

Furniture, household goods, cars, gadgets, even garbage trucks have a modern, fresh design. These days, attractive design is also a consideration in everything from factory construction to software, and of course, it is customizable. Good design is more than an aesthetic appearance. It finds solutions that the customer sees are well thought out and that make the product easy to use. Can this be expressed in sales figures? Think about Apple, Mini, Dyson or KitchenAid.

**Ask others if the product design is future-proof:**

- Key clients
- New clients
- Employees

As a product manager, do not create the design yourself. This is someone else's core competence, even if you would find it really fun.

Go to a professional design agency and find out what services it can offer you. Let them show you design solutions and explain the initial goal, what considerations went into the solution and how the goals were reached. Take a look at the sample and decide for yourself if the agency could implement your requirements.

**Modern design finds well-thought-out solutions:**

- Integration of new technologies
- User friendliness
- Good ergonomics
- Energy efficiency
- Simple construction

The possibilities are significant. You can minimize the production costs and still sell a noticeably better design. Take a look at the IF Award and RedDot Design Award websites. You'll be astonished which industries strive for ingenious designs. Maybe there's a company from your sector there too?

Play with the Luddites. Give them the cheaper company car, old office furniture, or plastic cups instead of porcelain at the next company meeting. If you get dismissive reactions, you're in a strong position. Then begin with a modern design development.

It is an extraordinary experience when longtime critical salesmen and employees have things like "That product is sexy!" "It is a lot of fun to work with this machine," or "The customers are stunned" to say about a new product in the factory.

**Have you thought of some possibilities to improve the product design? Write your actions on the last page.**

# 22. Present Convincingly

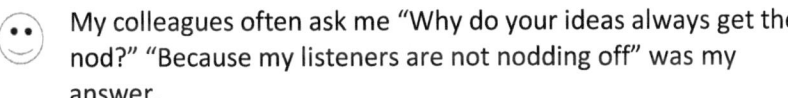 My colleagues often ask me "Why do your ideas always get the nod?" "Because my listeners are not nodding off" was my answer.

What did I do differently? I was prepared!

Many people do not like presentations and avoid them like crowded buses. But sometimes there is no next bus coming: You have to get in.

Presenting is to enthuse fast with a splash. I can assure you that this is something you can learn. But before you sign up for a rhetoric seminar, I will show you ways to plan your next presentation more effectively and convince your listeners.

**Before the presentation, ask yourself:**

- Which listeners have the decision-making power?
- What values and mindsets do the participants have?
- What are the listeners expecting from the presentation?
- What information will surprise the audience?
- How can I suit my arguments to the audience?
- What facts support my arguments?

- Is all my information understandable to everyone?
- What visual aids can I use?
- What stories can I tell?

The answers will help you structure the content and explain your reasoning. They will make you more self-confident and show that you're trustworthy. You are becoming a thought leader!

Even if you have to present something spontaneously, use a few of these answers to help you present the information effectively. No one would deny you three minutes' preparation time if it means they'll have the information at the upcoming meeting. According to a study by the Wall Street Journal, 3% of presentations are inspiring, 13% are okay, 40% are soporific and 44% are boring! The following tips will put you in that 3% that inspires.


**Presenting for your listeners and the decision-makers:**

- Sell your knowledge ("My studies show", "My customers demand")
- Mention the background to the solution
- Explain the benefits for the client/customer
- Show images that evoke suitable emotions
- Use visual aids: samples, prototypes, design sketches, demos
- Let the audience feel/smell/use/listen
- Use flip charts during the presentation

Decision-makers take note of the presenter's manner and appearance as well. As we were exchanging experiences during a seminar, one participant complained that "New ideas never get past the committee. Everyone on the decision-making committee is incompetent." After several questions, it turned out that the presenter likes to call other people incapable, showing it in gestures and facial expressions and becoming very impatient if they do not understand his mathematical models. So, pay attention to your attitude as well as your presentation skills.

## 10 PowerPoint Presentation killers

1. Unstructured content
2. Small font
3. Complicated tables
4. Bright colors
5. Poor contrast
6. Too much information on a slide
7. Too many bullet points
8. Reading aloud from the slides
9. Technical jargon
10. Monotone style

## 11 tips for a presentation that customer will love:

1. Show excitement. It's contagious!
2. Allow yourself the luxury of having your own opinion
3. Add a touch of humor. Everyone likes to laugh and they will remember it
4. Use targeted questions to bring your listeners in
5. Ask questions that the listeners can answer with 'yes'
6. Introduce your topic by telling a personal story
7. Find common ground: "We all..."
8. Speak without notes and keep eye contact
9. Take 3–5 second pauses while speaking to emphasize important information
10. Use short sentences (8 words max) to build excitement
11. Use action words and the present tense

An example of a typical line from a presentation:
Last year, we had a big revenue gain. The retailers have told us that the end users will be satisfied with the new product and that last year's results will be exceeded.

How does the following wording sound to you:
2016. (Pause) 5% revenue gain. Retailers say the current product is selling spectacular. With the long-awaited product our increase will be 8%. (Slowly write only '8%' on a flip chart. Pause for 3 seconds before the second sentence.) Feel the attention that you're creating!

Learn to wake up and captivate your listeners with positive expressions and facts. How inspirational are the words 'good' and 'new' to you? What emotions to the following words trigger with you?

**Examples of positive expressions:**

phenomenal, exceptional, impressive, crystal clear, astonishing, spectacular, irresistible, long awaited, convincing, tempting

## 23. Market Data in Brief – The PM's Cockpit

A CEO once said to me "I prefer to talk to my customers and then make decisions. All the analyses take too long to complete." Was he right?

He is a brave person and sees wrong decisions as a chance to learn. However, he still needs some market data. Can you imagine when he wants to read it? Yesterday!

That is why it is helpful if you get the relevant market data for your product portfolio before you need it.

**Relevant information for a product management (PM) cockpit:**

- Knowledge of the company strategy and goals
- Sales and turnover figures
- Revenue of product and line
- Total turnover share of product/product line
- Most important competitors and their best sellers

Regularly update and get information from other departments. Store the information in such a way that you can quickly find it again. Create a presentation template or use a database or software that creates one automatically.

Software tools that support a PM cockpit:

www.dashboardzone.com/

www.tableau.com

www.demandmetric.com

# 24. Avoid Conflicts: Appreciation

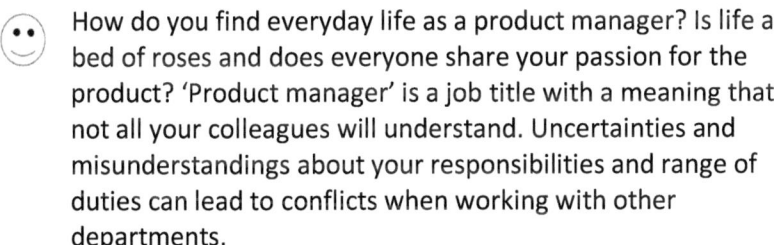 How do you find everyday life as a product manager? Is life a bed of roses and does everyone share your passion for the product? 'Product manager' is a job title with a meaning that not all your colleagues will understand. Uncertainties and misunderstandings about your responsibilities and range of duties can lead to conflicts when working with other departments.

A customer told me this typical reaction to a product manager: "Now my product manager even wants to tell me how I should bake my own bread." A product manager has to leave the beaten path and go somewhere new, but others may fear and reject new things.

**Together instead of against each other – what helps?**

- Understanding each other's tasks and responsibilities
- Pointing out the company's common goals
- Cross-divisional cooperation
- Understanding about the tasks of other departments
- Expressing the value, in words and in emails, of colleagues' experience
- Praising others for their performance
- Criticizing respectfully and with suggestions for improvement
- Showing patience with changes in processes and innovations

**Marketing for your own product management**

- Presenting the department on the intranet/black board
- Publishing articles in the company magazine
- Active participation in employee and trade events

**What steps can you take to avoid future conflicts? Write your ideas on the last page.**

## 25. A Symbiosis with the Sales Department

Q When do you speak with the sales managers or team?

☺ When organizing the management of a product, the sales department must be very closely integrated into the development process. It often happens that the sales department does not have enough, or even any, information about new products. And the sales personnel offer the new products only reluctantly.

Why do we keep hearing about trench warfare between the product management and the sales staff? The sales person is of inestimable value to the product management. He goes to the customer, knows the concerns and needs of the retailers and customers, and knows which products are bestsellers, which are flops, and what sales pitches will find a sympathetic ear with the customers. On the other hand, without product managers or developers there would not be any products to sell.

Recognize and use the advantages of both groups to optimize your processes. Communicate better and work together towards your goal: More sales of products that delight the customers.

**Making communication happen**

- Attend sales meetings regularly
- Present new product ideas and marketing campaigns
- Keep the sales team informed about the product roadmap
- Include the sales department in decisions throughout the product lifecycle
- Visit customers together
- Proactively mention customer visits
- Get market sales figures on a regular basis
- Ask for country reports
- Create training material in good time
- Train the sales personnel before the market launch
- Get feedback about the market launch

This is how you show interest in the sales team's experience while adding to your market knowledge. The sales department gets the information they need on time and can clarify points with the buyers if necessary. However, it is important to ensure that the information remains confidential. No one should make promises to customers about a product that cannot be kept.

## 26.Fair Prices at Last – Setting Prices

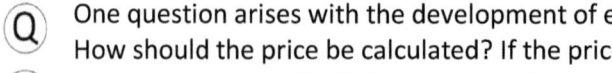 One question arises with the development of every product: How should the price be calculated? If the price is too high, the product may not sell. If it is too low, so is the company's revenue.

Calculate the product costs and the costs of extra services over the entire product lifecycle to avoid surprises with the margin. Ask your potential customers what they expect and try to adjust the prices accordingly. Most consumers will spend more if all of their needs are met. Do not worry that only low prices will be mentioned – "Tight is not always right!"

How can you calculate the price that's right for the customer?

**Setting customer-oriented prices:**

- Find out what features are important to your customers
- What stops your customers from buying your product or similar products from the competition?
- Segment customers according to their different wishes and then set the prices
- Search for alternative solutions (products and services) that work with the different prices
- Consider the different purchasing power of different target groups or regions

Price transparency means that a customer can understand the reasons for a particular price, be it uniqueness, bleeding edge technology or fair-trade production. Customers are very well informed these days and can usually choose products from a variety of vendors. That is why they need an understanding of the reason for the price.

An example of a lack of transparency is the price increase of the social network Xing. In March 2014, Xing significantly raised their prices for Swiss premium users. Instead of €128.30, the

Swiss customer was asked to pay more than 286 CHF for a 2-year subscription. In the email information, the currency conversion from the Euro to the Swiss franc was given as a reason. Hardly any customers could understand this price increase and many were upset. A Xing-Fail protest group was even started on Twitter!

This is not to say that you should reveal your product price calculation. The price calculation stays a business secret. What is important is that the customer feels comfortable with the price and services. If customers do not understand the price, none of your arguments will come to anything and the customers will look elsewhere.

## 27. Prices are Emotional – Always!

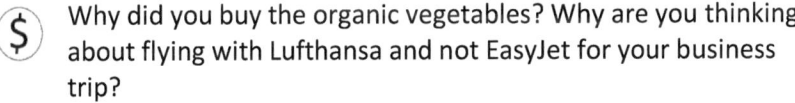

Why did you buy the organic vegetables? Why are you thinking about flying with Lufthansa and not EasyJet for your business trip?

Because you have certain expectations and wishes! The unconscious is directly reflected in the price we expect to pay.

**Unconscious influences on price:**

- Basic demands about quality, design, price, functionality, service, ecology, humanity, image
- Recommendations from trusted third parties
- Previous experience with the company or its competition
- Experiences with a similar product
- Reviews on internet comparison services, e.g. www.comparis.chciao.co.uk, www.kelkoo.co.uk, www.consumer.ftc.gov
- consumer reports i.e. www.consumerreports.org, www.testingmagazine.com,

We unconsciously take these factors into account when purchasing a product and comparing prices. For everything from consumer goods to capital investments, the customer decides whether the price is justified given his expectations.

**Benefit-oriented customers** do not buy a drill or a cell phone because the product has a beautiful design. They pay the price if the product's functionality meets their needs. These customers love test reviews.

**Service-oriented customers** appreciate being able to choose between different services and only pay for them if they use them. An example is when shipping is available in 'normal', 'fast' or 'urgent'. Airlines do it too: economy, business, first class. Each segment meets a specific demand, e.g. cheap, flexible or more comfortable. Service-oriented customers tend to consider the recommendations and experiences of their friends.

**Price-oriented customers** will be delighted with a product if you offer promotions or sales.

Emotions even come into play with technical goods: In this case, the emotions decide according to precision, reliability, perfection or improvements. For financial products, the emotions decide according to trust, security, relationship management, and individual service. Recognize the actual value of the product and emotions.

## 28. "Want to bet that...?"

### ... by tomorrow you will love advertisements?

The phone rings, and the sales manager, Mr. Drizzle, is angry about the latest product because of the staggering number of shopkeeper complaints. You have a sinking feeling, because as a product manager, you want happy customers. You are not alone with this feeling. Most people find complaints uncomfortable. But it does not have to be that way.

**Change your perspective:**

You receive a phone call. Someone is taking the time to contact you and to tell you about his problems.

**Complaints give you free information about:**

- Quality defects
- Incorrect use
- The users
- Opportunities for improvement

**Tips for dealing with complaints:**
- Take a deep breath!
- Draw a smiley face on a piece of paper and smile back at it!
- Have the caller tell you as much as possible about the product or service
- Ask clear and specific questions
- Find out about the next steps
- Include the complainant as a future test person
- Call the complainant after the complaint has been processed and ask him if he is satisfied

As a product manager, you will receive complaints: from the executive board, production, sales department, or key customers. A positive attitude makes friendly conversation and the search for a solution easier.

## 29. Marketing for Technicians

Technicians and engineers love facts, facts, facts! They'd prefer to sell products by describing functions, dimensions, and technological highlights. But do car lovers buy a Porsche because it has 315 horsepower, or because it sounds and feels good? Why does a biker buy a Harley Davidson in Germany? Why do women own an average of 20–30 pairs of shoes?

Marketing is not "incomprehensible and a waste of money." It is the art of attracting the customer's unconscious. Marketing is essential for companies of all sizes and industries.

**Marketing is everything - or do your customers buy directly from the factory?**

- Online presence (website, social media)
- Business cards
- Flyers and brochures
- Exhibition stands
- Personalities and expertise
- Word of mouth advertisement
- Networking events
- Lectures and training
- Points you make in the sales process
- Product appearance and functionality
- Product sound (think of potato chips or the noise of a Porsche)

You can win or lose customers with everything.

**For sales documents, sales information or marketing activities, remember the following:**

- Identify the concrete solution that brings more pleasure and less frustration when using the product or service
- Talk about longings or the fulfillment of wishes

- Show what will happen if the product or service is not used anymore
- Appeal to the five senses
- Do not use hackneyed marketing phrases
- Think about what else you can offer the customer
- Offer product samples or calculation sheets (B2B) that facilitate decision making

**Two real examples from the marketing department for kitchen knives:** Zwilling®, Damaskus (2014)

*"Authentic, unique, pure.*
*A UNIQUE OBJECT OF DESIRE. Larding and garnishing knife 100 mm (4")."*

Kaji, Utility Knife (2014)

*"The Kaji utility knife is perfect for use in the kitchen. For preparation or for longer jobs, everything can be done with the Kaji utility knife."*

*The polished Damascus blade and the handle of fine, laminated pakka wood, complete the Kaji utility knife.*

Try to find out what inspires your customers and how to keep them long term.

**Questions for efficient marketing:**

- What customer processes can be simplified?
- What information and what services can we use to exceed customers' expectations?
- What helps the customer to save time or money?
- What works really well and how can that be reinforced?
- How does the product improve the customer's image?

**Ask your customers directly:**

- How would you rate our sales service?
- Do you feel understood by us?
- What service is important to you?
- What else would you like from us?
- Why did you decide on us?
- What would make you switch to the competition?

**Have you identified an opportunity to market your products better to your target customers? Then write the actions you will take on the last page!**

## 30. Determine Customer Satisfaction

A customer's satisfaction with a product or a service is what decides whether he stays loyal to the company, recommends the services, or complains. You have no doubted heard of a 'shitstorm' in which the social media comments of a lot of dissatisfied customers have massively hurt the image of a company. More frequently you will find product recalls from big enterprises such as Mars, VW, Samsung, Merk, Boeing.

A customer is satisfied with a product if his expectations for the product are fulfilled after the purchase. Such a customer will gladly recommend the product or the service. You generate true enthusiasm if you, as the company, can offer the customer more than he expected. With this 'wow effect', customers will do word of mouth advertising of their own accord.
Look at the many enthusiastic customers of 'toto washlets' on YouTube.

However, a satisfied client will not always remain satisfied. Features or services that are now 'attractive', can become merely standard tomorrow. Innovative, modern customers find these standards unspectacular.

**5 ways to check customer satisfaction:**

1. Key figures for customer satisfaction, e.g. repurchasing rate, revenue per customer, willingness to recommend, complaint processing time, etc.
2. Categorize customer wishes as excitement factors, functionality preferences, and basic requirements. This gives you information about customer loyalty and recommendations.
3. For sophisticated products, structured customer interviews asking about experiences and a detailed description of the situation.
4. Analysis of complaints by the after-sales team: what were the most common complaints and how many were there?
5. Evaluation of the guarantee: For which products were warranty services most needed?

Customer satisfaction questionnaires are anonymous, widely applicable and popular because they cost little and can be answered without outside influence. Creating a survey is by no means trivial. The right questions, the combination of questions, and the possible answer choices are important for both data entry and analysis. If you decide to use a questionnaire, try it on different test people first. This lets you check functionality and clarity of the questions in advance and, if necessary, correct them.

However, the response rate of questionnaires is usually very low. Anonymous customer surveys usually have a response rate of about 0.5%. The response rate for existing customers can be

5% or higher. You can increase the response rate with a thank-you to the participants. A suitable thank-you could be the results of the survey, a small gift, a sample, or a book on the topic.

For more information about designing surveys, visit www.surveygizmo.com, www.surveymonkey.com, www.typeform.com, http://www.amplituderesearch.com/, www.survey-design-and-analysis.com/customer-panels

# Your Actions

---

---

---

---

---

---

---

---

---

---

---

---

---

---

---

---

---

Thank you for buying "A Product Manager's Cookbook".

You can share experiences with me, or give some feedback

to ulrike.laubner@corimbus.ch.